Profile 5 – MARY LOHAN

Profile 5 – MARY LOHAN

Published as part of Gandon Editions'
PROFILES series on Irish artists (details p47).

ISBN 0946641 889

Editor   John O'Regan

Asst Editor   Nicola Dearey
Design   John O'Regan
                (© Gandon, 1997)
Production   Gandon
Photography   Gillian Buckley
                (except pp26-27 by
                John Searle)
Printing   Nicholson & Bass, Belfast

Distributed by Gandon and its overseas agents

GANDON EDITIONS
Oysterhaven, Kinsale, Co Cork
tel +353 (0)21-770830 / fax 770755

cover   *Misty Morning,*
                Gweebarra Bay (1997)

Publication grant-aided by
The Arts Council / An Chomhairle Ealaíon

The Arts Council
An Chomhairle Ealaíon

Prof le

Mary Lohan

GANDON EDITIONS

World = Paint

AIDAN DUNNE

A SALIENT FEATURE OF MARY LOHAN'S PAINTINGS IS THE WAY THAT THEIR PHYSICAL BOUNDARIES mark the borders of a preserve within which everything is substantially the same. Given that her dominant subject is landscape, and that we can usually distinguish land from sea, sea from sky in any given picture, it might seem perverse to say this. But the common horizon is paint. This is not merely a question of semantics, a factual observation that an oil painting is primarily a thin skin of coloured pigment on a prepared support. In her work, the data of the external world are comprehensively translated into the substance of paint. Land equals paint. Sky equals paint. Sea equals paint.

Even if we leave paint out of the equation for a moment, it is possible to envisage circumstances that contain clues as to how the world might be experienced in something like this way. It is characteristic of many parts of Ireland's rural landscape that there are days when the air is so laden with moisture and the ground so waterlogged that it seems as if they are related states of the same substance, the same stuff that we happen to be sampling in different forms as solid, liquid and gas – not quite ice, water and vapour, but pretty close. It is like a form of synaesthesia in which all the senses blend into one enveloping receptivity. Comparable

5

experiences of environment might come through an activity like diving or gliding. Peter Lanyon's paintings were certainly informed by his flying, and James Turrell identifies flight as central to his perceptions, speaking of swimming in an ocean of air.

As for paint: when Nicolas Poussin planned his immensely formalised compositions, he often made elaborate, stage-lit studio models. This partly explains how he transmuted the various elements in his stoic dramas – including the human players – into a single medium. The sky, each deep-focus, recessive layer of landscape, every calculated classical ruin, the poised *dramatis personae*, all are of a piece. Every portion of the picture surface is evenly, calmly treated. The compositional structure and the skin of the painting knit them all together as surely as if we are looking at one integral organism. The same impulse is evident in Cézanne's landscapes, when he translates everything, including the spaces between things – the air itself – into a language of blocky forms. In other words, nothing, in Cézanne's physics, has the same weight as something.

It is now many years since Lohan painted the human figure. When she did so, much the same description applied as to her treatment of landscape. That is to say, the pigment embodied flesh, and the distinction between figure and ground dissolved. Similarly, her paintings of both buildings and flowers resist any view of either as isolated objects. Nothing suggests that she will not paint the figure or flowers or buildings again at some stage in the future, but the trend in her work might be described as having been from a hierarchical pattern of subject and ground to a democratic one in which no distinct, iconic motif is allowed to dominate.

There is another trend worth noting, and that is one towards increasing thicknesses of paint. It is not a straightforward progression. Even in her gouache studies of flowers she shows signs, within the limits of the medium, of using the paint thickly. When she used oil initially, she continued to work on paper, a support that also placed constraints on the sheer quantity of pigment. Since starting to work on various kinds of wood support, she has consistently painted fairly thickly, sometimes less

so, sometimes more, but on the whole, she uses, in relative terms, a lot of paint.

This has to do partly with how she makes her pictures. She works exclusively with knives and scrapers – painting knives and flexible scrapers. It is not exclusively an additive process, and it is not uncommon for virtually all the pigment to be scraped off a work in progress, leaving just the blurred foundation layer. It is clear that this has to happen at least occasionally given that she paints wet on wet: when a picture is in the making, she must be able to attack any part of the surface to any depth of paint. While this allows her to develop ranges of homogeneous, densely blended colours, soupy, viscous textures, and the infinite tonal subtlety that is characteristic of her paintings, it also means that if things go awry, there is no way of fixing them bar starting again.

So, to some extent, working methods determine the thickness of paint, but by no means entirely. Without a doubt, many works seem to reflect her desire that they should be substantial physical objects. As with the figure paintings, this may have to do with embodiment, with finding a painterly equivalent for and acknowledging the complicated materiality of the experienced world. But it may equally and simultaneously relate to an insistence on a painting's status as a distinct, autonomous object in its own right. There's certainly a tension there that she chooses to exploit rather than resolve.

It is not the only inbuilt contradiction. Underlying the sheer weight of pigment in the paintings, there is also an awareness of ceaseless change: the tides vary in their daily cycle, the clouds crank across the sky, one season gives ground to the next. And the sum of these myriad, interconnected shifts and cycles is a perpetual restlessness. Light and shadow, colour, texture, mass, mood itself are in a state of flux. Looking at any particular painting, you're aware that numerous drafts are fixed in its mass of underlying and up-ended layers, like rock strata. It's a nexus of processes that happens to be stilled in one particular configuration, shaped, perhaps, by something as evanescent as a flicker of light bouncing off the wave peaks, the glistening rocks, the flat estuarine muds. Sculptural impasto sets fugitive details as if they have been cast in bronze. But when a painting arrives at its destination, though it's there to stay, there is still an intimation of transience. Natural mutability finds a counterpart in the potential plasticity of the paint surface.

Generally, Lohan's favoured terrains are ones shaped by the elements. But the remotest places also have a human history. Take Port, an interesting example because it represents, she remarks, more or less everything she looks for in a landscape. Strikingly situated at the mouth of a valley on the north-west of the Slieve League Peninsula in Donegal,where the rocky coastline tumbles into the pounding waves, Port was inhabited. On the valley's gentler, northern slope, there are ruined cottages and boundary walls, and the corrugations of lazy beds. The ubiquitous sheep hug the rough road and fan out on to the hillside. Further back up the valley, a handful of houses are habitable, though just one is permanently occupied. A few lobster fishermen work from the harbour. But it is an unforgiving environment, and what was a small community moved out as far back as the early nineteenth century, according to one local source, and relocated to more accessible places, better served with amenities.

That seems to be pretty much Lohan's kind of place. People impinge, because that's what humans do. But they take in the dark surface of Lough Kiltyfanned, the forbidding north-facing slab of mountainside behind it, a scene which might as well have a sign saying, 'There's Nothing For You Here', and on the whole, they would rather be in Philadelphia. And, but for the discarded oil bottles and other debris, the sheep, people looking for and sometimes taken aback by solitude, Port is really left pretty much to itself and the seabirds.

To base paintings on this location might in itself be described as a nostalgic gesture when the overwhelming majority of the population lives in cities and is primarily familiar with a man-made urban environment and a virtual, electronically generated one, when the very notion of 'nature' has been dismissively analysed as a sentimental cultural construct. But despite its air of unpopulated wilderness, Lohan's work does not hinge on a nostalgic, mythical view of an untouched, virgin nature. Rather the sense we get from her landscapes is that what we habitually call nature is always contingent. Continents fracture, drift, collide; mountain ranges are thrown up; landmasses are raised, eroded, sculpted, contorted, drowned, broken; plant and animal communities flourish and fade. The only precedence nature possesses is that this is the way things are. This happens to be the world we find ourselves in. It is essentially indifferent to our presence.

The paintings do, however, articulate and offer us spaces with which we can engage, that we might like to explore. And, in a way, they subordinate us to these often spectacular spaces, not by invoking notions of the sublime, but by giving us walk-on parts in a greater, not remotely terrifying drama. Lohan does not try to induce awe with vertiginous views of plunging sea cliffs and cloud-mantled peaks. Nor do the pictures appeal to romantic ideas of a picturesque, remote, depopulated West. What counts is not the location in that sense – she will paint much more contained environments, like garden and park, in exactly the same spirit – but the relationship between the painter and, standing in for the painter, the viewer, with the space that the paintings make available. Inevitably, there is a sense of landscape as a congeries of meanings, as being significant to individuals. But those meanings are not spelled out.

Perhaps one of the things Lohan's paintings do is to appeal to a certain shared way of viewing landscape, one that is tied up with memory in a general sense, in the popular imagination. For many people, coastal landscapes are privileged through their specific association with holidays, summer and freedom. Of course, there are a whole range of other associations; for example, the sea is also immensely threatening. But the shore is overwhelmingly an imaginative threshold, not a place of escape, but one of confrontation with self. In positing an openness to environment, an unrestrained curiosity, the paintings in some way echo the way a child can relate to landscape – as a realm of pure possibility.

Aidan Dunne is an art critic for the *Sunday Tribune* and has written extensively on Irish art.

The Lie of the Land

Words adjacent to the paintings of Mary Lohan

NOEL SHERIDAN

WHAT A WONDERFUL AND STRANGE PLACE IT IS THIS 'LAND OF PAINT' AND EVERYONE WHO PAINTS wants to get there. You get into it as much by touch as by sight. How heavy or light the touch, how considered or spontaneous the hand movement, what freight of colour or viscosity of pigment gets carried on the journey begins to settle this land. You make a beginning so you can start to look. Then you travel. Where you want to go is a place you have never been before, yet you sense that when you arrive it will be a place you seem to know. What makes it familiar is something from the past and also something of the future – a promise. But the main thing about this land – what makes it art – is that it must be made to exist, palpably, in its own time present. As authentic as a tea cup, taking its time and space in ours. Begin.

As the painting starts to insist on its space occupying your space, you negotiate an uneasy contract between you and it, which sets the lie of this land. Touch and look your way into it. Then continue the looking for a long time. Nothing gets your concentrated attention like this; your eyes are peeled. You keep looking for a long time, until everything is radiant, significant. Yes, it looks interesting. Then you look at the floor; that now looks equally radiant, significant and interesting. More interesting because it is *really* in the world, part of it, authentic, stupifyingly real. Not a representation, not a blueprint, nothing at a remove, but right there, now. This is what you want the paint to be. But you are seeing too much. This is raw seeing, the life-pits before art. The half of painting that is pain begins to operate here. Begin again.

Touch our way in, scraping, layering, digging out, plastering on, scraping off. Looking, looking. The eye skating on it, sinking into it. There are two speeds. The first slick and shiny; the eye races across the paint surface, skidding away. The second, glutinous, slow motion lava; tracing the imperceptible movement and growth of stone. Ancient, lithic, grey... Stop. Just paint.

Bring light to this place. Everything receives light but painting contends that light; trapping it so that this dumb, resilient, buttery paint seems to radiate a light of itself. It is the hopeless faith in that impossibility that makes this land of paint so human, touching and sometimes amazing.

> The worst is not over, yet I know
> You will be happy here. Because of the logic
> Of your situation, which is something no climate can outsmart.
> Tender and insouciant by turns, you see
>
> You have built a mountain of something.
> Thoughtfully pouring all your energy into this single monument,
> Whose wind is desire starching a petal,
> Whose disappointment broke into a rainbow of tears.
>
> — John Ashbury, *These Lacustrine Cities*

Take heart from the cliche 'dumb as a painter'. Speech merely flutters its wings against the surface of this medium. Press on. Remember that concepts such as 'landscape' are merely hooks to memory that steady the eye. What traps and holds the eye is an adhesiveness special to this place of paint. It is another world and part of getting into it comes with the realisation that, as you look at it, *it is looking at you*. (If everyday things in the world start to look at you, something is wrong; if painting does not do it, something is wrong.)

Look how it looks. That sweeping scan of stops and glides that sometimes stall to saturation; glimpses that flick as highlights,

slow searches that drag across the surface only to be turned as trammels that impede, spur and lift to hover forever. This is a look to which even time cannot bring repose – for time is what is missing from this land. It is language that unfolds in time; in this place of space, 'time has turned into space and there will be no more time.' (Beckett, *Text for Nothing*)

Consider scale. Whether we see this land as detail or panorama – it could be either – is incidental to the size and scale of the painting itself. Sometimes you get the small, one-shot size; you see it in one take. These are like babies and they hold the fascination of babies; designed for success, even small 'peculiarities' seem full of promise. All seems nascent, full of broiling potential and they are the ideal size for the eye to hold and feed. When they get bigger they demand attention at the uneasy periphery of vision. They are more unpredictable. We want these unruly adolescents – or curmudgeonly elders – to simply stay in the frame that is our conceptual frame. It should be landscape but it's paint; it should be paint but it's behaving like weather; it makes sense now – close up – but what is it doing over there, and now where is it going? These paintings are grown-ups – you don't so much understand as accept them – and look at the time they take; they are not so easily accommodated by the eye and brain that must now give time and thought to come to terms with the fact that this moiling mass, macro or micro, will be eternally

> ... causing some features palpably nearer your pecker to be swollen up most grossly while the further back we manage to wiggle the more we need the loan of a lens to see as much as the hen saw. Tip.
>
> — Joyce, *Finnegans Wake*

And besides, you can't help thinking – *if only you could stop thinking* – this is a bad time to be painting. It is as incorrect as the Full Irish Breakfast – and for many of the same reasons. Blood, ghee, muscle and brains condensed into a life-threatening assault on the system is dangerous. It could be a matter of life and death; the risk-level is high; you are taking terrible chances. And what has life, death, risk and chance to do with art? That was then. Modernism. Read today's menu: 'Vegetarian sausage with just a hint of hickory'. That weasel 'hint of' points modishly to the fact that you probably have the wrong agenda.

But you know, you just feel, that deep down what everyone wants is the art equivalent of the FIB: the Velazquez, the Goya, the Vuillard, the de Stael, the Guston, the de Kooning, the Reubens, and, yes, the Bacon. The full edible listing. The Ates.

Turn back from these trophic metaphors; they lead to the same queasy euphoria that confuses the floor with the painting. What is needed now is something to prevent the painting becoming linoleum; more cover-up than real. You have reached that place of excavation in this land where you realise that in order to go forward or back, the floorboards have to come up. Now, there is only deeper. You have buried the natural light of the blank board where those original marks danced and took their first breaths. You have layered and pulled and tried to save lovely passages that finally had to go under because the logic of this place had begun to take a different turn. This has led you into ever-darker dullness where everything seems to die under your hand. Thick and synthetic as lino, it bends and buckles, its light has gone. It can be designed now anyway you push it. It gives, but there is no take. There is no resistance. This is the terror of abstraction; how to stop it being interior design. Yet, where you are now, numbed in this paintland, needs design, craft; something that works. What do you know from the past that might revive it?

Salmon pink will never again travel as miraculously as it did across the silver-grey of the small Infanta's dress, but try. There will never be touch like that again, but go on. Not under or over but *on* and *in*. Does that help? Look. Maybe that pink has brought something flickering to life. Believe it. Begin again.

What a wonderful and strange place this is. You think you may now know this place because you have traversed it some time ago and traces remain of your having been there. You have shifted things and things have shifted you. You recognise things you made happen but most interesting are things that just happened and… just appeared out of this land. These are the events that constitute the reason you do this.

Still, elements feel wrong. (Like 'constitute'. What you want is 'consistency' – in the medium that is – like 'sinewy'. No, that's wrong too. Go back. Erase. And lose the breakfast section. Won't fit. And that part about pictures looking was wrong. Try again.)

It is not that the painting looks at you – it is usually too involved with itself for that – but, if you get into this land, it will show signs of your looking out. This is called style.

Press on past these ideas of signs and style. They must emerge, occur. If you carry their freight into this land, they will hang out and then self-consciously wander the place like bleating sheep, cute and lost. Think dumb, then maybe, if you have truly entered this land of paint, and if you are lucky, there will be a moment when you feel you can't make a mistake. You may be wrong, but something of your stuff and its stuff has arrived. Don't ask where it came from, just pinch its cheeks, brush its hair, straighten its dress. It's behaving itself. Maybe you can now send it out into the world. (An act of faith, of course, but how sustaining it is – as good as the floor – the lie of this land.)

This now is something from the land of paint. It has light. Look at it looking. Thoughtfully pouring all of your energy into this single monument, you have signed off on this contract. You will be happy here. There is a logic to this place. Lighten up.

'The Vision of Mac Conglinne'

Haunch of Mutton
Is my dog's name
Of lovely leaps.

— from the 6th-century Irish

Noel Sheridan is director of the National College of Art and Design, Dublin, an art critic and artist

A Conversation with the Artist

AIDAN DUNNE

Aidan Dunne – I have noticed that you have a lot of photographs in the studio. Do you use them a lot when you paint?

Mary Lohan – I do and I don't. I take a lot of photographs but I'm not a photographer. They're not good photographs. When I am out walking, I bring a camera and I try to capture what I see, but I find it never really works. The photograph never captures what I have in mind. But they are useful to me. I use them as memory aids. They're not totally necessary, though.

What do you try to get in a photograph?

The kind of feeling that is in the paintings, but I don't. When I'm in the country, I get totally excited by what I see, and I have this desire to capture it and bring it back to the studio. As a process, it seems to have its own logic. I have also worked on the spot – I've made paintings out there, when I've been in Donegal – but for some reason those paintings often do not work. If I can somehow bring back the experience to the studio and work on it there, to paint it from inside, then I seem to be able to attain some approximation of what it was like.

When you say 'inside', do you mean inside the studio ... and 'out there' is the landscape?

By 'out there' I mean you are painting what you are looking at in front of you. By 'inside' I do not mean in the studio, though it usually is in the studio, but that you are painting from an internalised experience. You are at a distance, so you are working from within yourself rather than checking something outside of yourself.

Most of your paintings picture a shoreline.

The sea is absolutely central to the paintings. I love it because it is this highly textured, ever-changing medium that plays with light. It is alive, it's constantly moving, the light is always shifting, it reflects the sky and the land, and it takes on the character of the sky and the land. I love tidal areas, expanses of mud and sand and stones that are covered and uncovered, sculpted by the water. In fact, my favourite time is when the tide is out.

I should say that I am also terrified of the sea. I have been ever since I was a child. It seems huge and threatening to me. I don't particularly like being in it or on it.

A lot of your paintings are of subjects in Donegal?

In Donegal there is the kind of space and the kind of shoreline that enabled me to see what I wanted to do in painting. But when I talk about Donegal, I wouldn't like to give the impression that I only paint Donegal. I have painted other places, like West Cork, North Mayo and Dublin. When I visit Dublin Bay, I get the same feeling about the landscape; it is just as exciting, just as interesting in many ways. For a while, I painted the city, up around Mountjoy Square where I had a studio. But I think Donegal is spectacular. There are wonderful spaces there.

My first show was entirely of flowers from my garden. It took me over two years to make that exhibition. People liked the paintings – I could have done it again. But for me the success of that show was like being given permission to paint. I bought oil paint and knives, and worked my way out into the Phoenix Park. It is a familiar place for me because I live beside it and have visited it all my life. I made paintings of trees and water.

And then Donegal. When I set out to paint in Donegal, for the first and probably the only time in my life I knew exactly what I was going to do, how I was going to do it, and what it should look like, which is kind of strange. In my second show, the sea did not figure at all. The paintings were green, green, green. I made a lot of paintings of the land along the Glen River. Then I visited Port, which is a pretty remote valley on the sea on the Slieve League peninsula. Port really has everything that is interesting for me in landscape, summer and winter.

You stayed on Tory Island as well?

Tory is amazing. I stayed there for three or four weeks. I was completely alone, so it seemed longer. It is an extraordinary, elemental landscape. There's actually very little land to speak of, and a great deal of sea; you are perched on these sea cliffs. The sea completely dominates the island. Every way you turn, it is there; it's very much in your face. I still do paintings based on that experience of Tory.

One thing that was particularly interesting for me was the idea of being in the same landscape over time. I have spent short periods of time in various places, particularly in Donegal, but what I haven't yet done, and would really like to do, is to follow a particular place through all the seasons. I believe your surroundings fundamentally affect you. Also, if I were in one place all the time, I would calm down a bit. I mean, there wouldn't be the same urgency to take in everything immediately.

The dominant format of your paintings used to be a single, squarish shape, but now you do more diptychs and triptychs.

I have always experimented with formats, and for a long time what I was doing seemed to call for that squarish shape. You would think, logically, that landscape calls for a more conventional landscape format, but whenever I used that shape, I wasn't that happy with the result. Gradually, I began to feel that I needed more room, the picture needed to continue. It wasn't a matter of scale, it was a question of proportion; it was to do with extending the space horizontally. But I also wanted to retain that squarish shape, and the solution was a pair or a set of panels side by side, which also allows me to move them around, to examine each piece separately and see how they stand up.

Does it ever strike you as odd that you paint landscapes without buildings or people but you live in the city?

That's such a corny question! It is something you always hear. Why shouldn't you be able to live in the city and paint landscape? You walk down the road and you're at the canal bank; go out the door and you're in the garden; and then there's the park. When you find that too enclosing, you go out into the rural landscape. But I would say that I do not have an emotional attachment to landscape in terms of my upbringing, for example. My memories of going to the country as a child are memories of discomfort, of outside loos and funny looking country butter. And I like to be comfortable; I'm a city person. In the country I was homesick. I cried and wished I was back home.

When my sister started going out with a Donegal man – whom she eventually married – I was in my teens, and we would go to Donegal on visits. But, strange as it may seem, I never thought of it as being the country, never mind in terms of painting. It was just a hugely social place; we went to have a ball. The truth is that I never really saw the landscape until I was in my late twenties or early thirties. Until you're ready for something you just won't see it; it won't mean anything to you. I only begin to know things when they come to me in some personal way, when they become important to me and I want to know. And, although Donegal has been an important source for me, again I don't actually have a strong emotional or sentimental identification with a particular landscape. It seems to me that the association between yourself and landscape is changing all the time. I don't see the landscape as an absolute, unvarying source, and the work is really about that evolving relationship rather than about the landscape in itself.

So did art interest you when you were at school?

I was one of those people who are good at life drawing. When I painted, I painted gaunt figures who were on the verge of death through starvation. I had a huge social conscience. I was that kind of teenager. It is something you go through in adolescence. You are more interested in yourself and probably in other people in that kind of idealistic way.

You went on to the National College of Art and Design?

Yes, straight from boarding school to NCAD. It is hardly surprising that I was miserable in college a lot of the time. I never really expressed myself while I was there. I was a shy person, and I found it intimidating. I would have to admit that during the last two years in college I did very little work. Looking back, what was good for me about college is that it must have given me some skills. But then, I am not all that sure that it did. I still cannot make a stretcher, or do any of those sorts of things. I had the urge to paint when I went there, but it actually took me years to discover the self-confidence I needed to do my own work, which, incidentally, is not to blame the college. I had to come around to things in my own time.

Do you not think everybody has to do that?

I think that college will suit some people temperamentally more than others. Yes, some people love joining things – they are team players. Perhaps college suits a particular kind of personality. The funny thing is that I love routine. But it has to be my own routine that I have set up, and I'm very inflexible on it, especially if I am away. I have to get up at a certain time and start work at a certain time, and I don't vary from it. Otherwise I just wander. In college I just wandered.

What did you do after college?

I taught for four years, at second level, and got on very well at it. And then I thought I should go back and do the Principles of Teaching course if I was going to keep teaching. Going back to do things like drawing and craft was a good experience. It got me drawing again. But ironically, after doing that and qualifying, I haven't taught since. *(continued on page 42)*

Black Church, Dublin
1989, oil on card, 86 x 79 cm

Port a Cabhalaigh, Donegal
1991, oil on board, 119 x 122 cm

Cove, Port
1991, oil on board, 38 x 41cm

Sea Shore, Donegal
1992, oil on board, 37 x 61 cm

Early Morning, Port
1991, oil on board, 38 x 41 cm

Port, Donegal
1991, oil on card, 79 x 76 cm

Belderrig
1994, oil on board, 61 x 61 cm

Bogagh, Donegal
1994, oil on board, 61 x 61 cm

Sand, Sea and Light, Mayo
1996, oil on board, triptych, each 41 x 41 cm

Cashel Beach
1995, oil on board, 61 x 61 cm

Silver Strand, Donegal
1996, oil on board, 81 x 81 cm

Loughras Beg Bay
1996, oil on board, diptych, each 41 x 41 cm

Evening Tide, Rossan Point I
1996, oil on board, diptych, each 46 x 62 cm

Evening Tide, Rossan Point II
1996, oil on board, diptych, each 46 x 62 cm

Dooey Beach I
1996, oil on board, diptych, each 41 x 42 cm

Dooey Beach II
1996, oil on board, diptych, each 53 x 51 cm

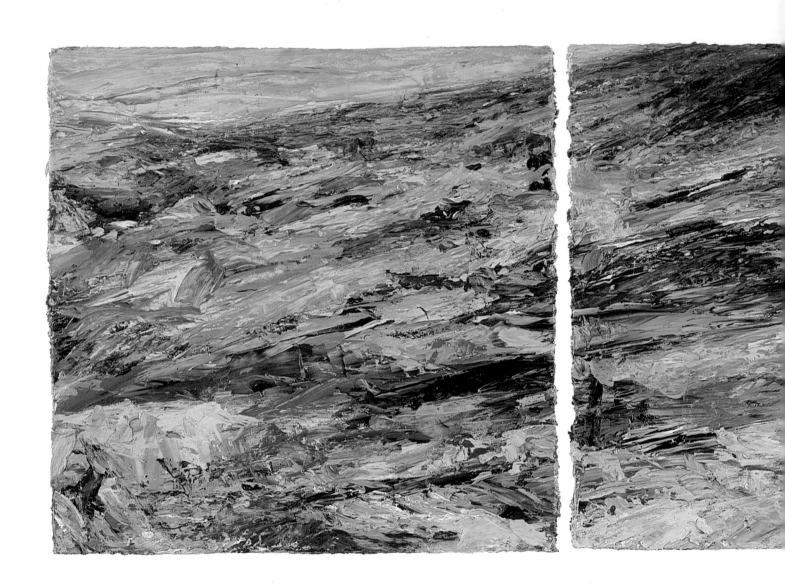

Strabuí, Donegal
1996, oil on board, triptych, each 41 x 41 cm

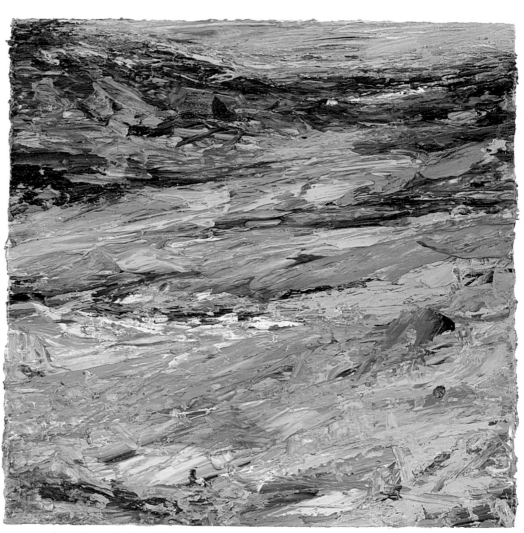

Rossan Point I
1997, oil on board, diptych, each 76 x 81 cm

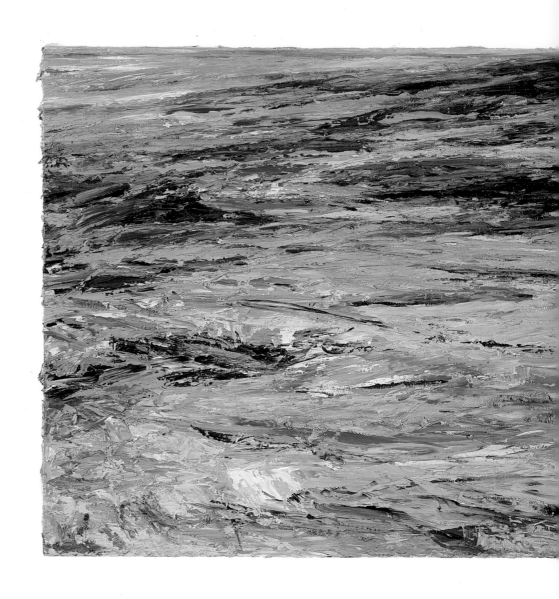

Rossan Point II
1997, oil on board, diptych, each 76 x 81cm

Arranmore I
1997, oil on board, diptych, each 41 x 51 cm

LIST OF ILLUSTRATIONS

all dimensions in centimetres – height precedes width

all photographs by Gillian Buckley, except pp26-27 by John Searle (continued from page 15) At that stage, I managed to get studio space in the Visual Arts Centre in Strand Street. There were good painters there, but I knew as soon as I walked into my space that it would be difficult for me. I felt as if I was back in college. There are so many painters who never went to college, and I still half-think that it is a bad thing to go. Yet the trend is towards a more and more academic emphasis. Perhaps it gives people a confidence in your work, like any other academic qualification, but I'm not so sure. As someone involved in art education said to me the other day, the students are all desperately worried over whether they get 2.1s or 2.2s, but, afterwards, you cannot arrive at the gallery door waving your degree saying you have to give me a show, look at my qualifications.

There was a break of several years before you began to paint?

Yes. Other things took over for a while. Having a family was important for me – I have two children, Mike and Geraldine.

What do you like about the process of painting?

I paint on the flat. I block in the colour, and then, in a way, the first exciting part of the process is when I lift the board onto the easel and have a look at it. You see a totally different image when you do that.

I like paint itself, lots of it. I would like vats of it. But I suppose any painter would, partly because you worry over practical things like the supply of materials. Painting itself is enjoyable, but it generates its own momentum and it can be deceptive. You get involved in it and think it is terrific. But of course you need time to judge. The more you look at a painting, the more likely you are to see what's right and wrong about it. So you spend a great deal of time looking at what you are doing. And it is important to leave it. The most useful gap is between one day and the next. You leave the studio thinking everything is sorted out, you've solved all the problems, there are no niggling little doubts. Next morning you walk in and you see huge gaps, and you realise you better roll up your sleeves.

You find yourself doing the same things again and again, like the painting I have on the easel now. I can see it is far too fussy. And it is not as if I haven't been here before. I wonder about that. It is as if you have to go through it. You lay down something and you know you're going to end up destroying it, it is not going to stay.

Why not just go straight to the final version?

I suppose there's something about knowing that there are other paintings underneath, that there is an underneath, a layering, a depth. It is almost like physically digging things up. I look at other people painting and I kid myself that I can do the same thing: lay out the colours, mix them, put them on in more or less the right order. But it doesn't work.

You never use colours direct from the tube, do you?

Almost never. Obviously I look for colours that are close to what I want, but even if I like a colour I find I have to modify it before I actually apply it. It's a personal thing. I see people using colour directly from the tube and it works perfectly well. But I feel I have to work. So when I get colours, I go for primaries and use them to adjust things like Paynes grey, Naples yellow, sap green and so on. I tend to go on and off colours. I'm currently reacting to the yellowy colours I was using before.

There are never any people in your paintings.

No. Why should there be people? The paintings deal with an aspect of the landscape. I wouldn't even say that I'm a landscape painter. I don't know that you can paint a landscape. You lose so much, depending on which line of approach you adopt. I would say I approach certain aspects of the landscape, and the way I approach it, there just couldn't be a person there. It has to be elemental. So it's for the same reason that I have no interest in something like the pattern of rooftops – that's all something else. They're about trying to get a space. The only person in them is me, me feeling part of the stuff of the painting.

People respond very warmly to your pictures, very emotionally. Does that ever surprise you?

It flabbergasts me that anyone does respond so warmly, and they do. But I do think the paintings are quite emotional. I think people respond to those things in them that label them as landscapes. The fact that there is a horizon line, a foreground, a middle ground. People can place themselves in relation to these things. In general, I find that people really like them or they do not like them at all.

If I were to ask myself what I like in them, it would be subtlety of colour, the bulk of paint. But I also like that it is a piece of board with some paint on it. That's all it is, yet somehow it might become something else as well. It will be either a lump of paint or an image – it's either there or it isn't.

You try to make an exciting surface. I do get uneasy when it becomes too literal. The horizon is a bit of a bogey. I often feel I would like to get rid of it, and I have done in some paintings. In a single panel, the horizon is less essential; in a wider format it seems to become inevitable.

If you're not a landscape painter as such, would you see yourself in relation to any Irish landscape tradition?

I would like to see myself in that context, but it is difficult to say it of yourself. I mean, I hardly see myself as a 'painter', and when someone asks me what paintings I really like, I find it difficult to think in those terms. I could probably count on the fingers of one hand the number of times I have really been moved by seeing a body of painting. The first time was an exhibition by Barrie Cooke. It was in the 1970s, and it was an exhibition based on the Burren. I was absolutely knocked out by those paintings, and it didn't even occur to me at the time that it was probably because I wanted to do something like that myself. Not that I see any direct connection between my work and his, but I have found his paintings really inspiring. I can remember coming away from a big show of his in the Douglas Hyde around the mid-1980s feeling really keen to get to work.

I have always liked the way Rothko painted, and Gorky; I wanted to paint like that. Then one day I remember going to the Municipal Gallery and seeing five paintings in a row by Nano Reid. I went back to look at them again and again. They were real landscapes, not the cat-on-the-mat stuff that you often see by her. She showed me that you could really do something with landscape. Until then, I had had a very negative view of her. Then I like some of Camille Souter and Paddy Collins. Not everything, but the moodiness. You see a lot of shows, and in the end you retain very little. Recently I was amazed at the Turners in the Clore – the way he uses white on white on white.

Two documentaries on painters have impressed me. One was on Tapies – whose work I really like – making a piece of work. The other was on Bill Crozier. I like that idea of seeing someone put a picture together. It tells you a lot. But in the end, when people ask what paintings have really affected me, and how, I can't honestly say. Often, say with Bonnard or Vuillard, what I really like are pieces of painting, how they apply the paint, how they put areas together. And sometimes seeing the scale is amazing. When I see a big Bonnard, I can't imagine painting that size.

Why not?

Because the larger I work the tighter I become, and also it becomes increasingly problematic – I would need a trowel to put the paint on! But I still have this feeling at the back of my mind that I would love the chance to work really big.

Do you think the density of paint in your work has to do with a sense of the past?

No. I think my paintings aren't about anything in that sense. They're about what I see and how I translate that into complications on a rectangular piece of board.

Is it an inexhaustible activity?

Yes. The last painting always suggests the next one. In fact, in the middle of a painting, you think of the next one. By the end, you're sure that you're ideally positioned to paint the painting you've just struggled with, but mentally you're partly inhabiting the next one.

MARY LOHAN

1954   Born in Dublin
1972-76 National College of Art and Design, Dublin
1979-80 NCAD, Dublin (Principles of Teaching)
1996-99 Member of the board of NCAD
         Lives and works in Dublin

Solo Exhibitions

1998   Galerie Médiart, Paris
         Taylor Galleries, Dublin
1995   *Sand, Sea and Light, Mayo*, Taylor Galleries, Dublin
1994   *Recent Paintings*, Grant Fine Art, Newcastle,
         Co Down
1993   *New Works on Paper*, Carroll Gallery, Longford
1992   *Elements*, Taylor Galleries, Dublin
         Donegal Landscapes, Model Arts Centre, Sligo
1991   *Donegal*, Taylor Galleries, Dublin
1990   *First Solo*, Riverrun Gallery, Dublin

Selected Group Exhibitions

1997   *Re-Dressing Cathleen*, McMullen Museum of Art,
         Boston College, Boston
         Maurice Desmond Selection, Lavit Gallery, Cork
         Critics' Choice, *Banquet Show,* RHA Gallagher
         Gallery, Dublin
1996   *l'Imaginaire Irlandais*, Galerie Médiart, Paris
         Living Landscape '96, West Cork Arts Centre,
         Skibbereen
1995   *Gwen O'Dowd and Mary Lohan*, West Cork Arts
         Centre, Skibbereen
         Claremorris Open Exhibition
         Banquet Show, RHA Gallagher Gallery, Dublin
1994   *Images of North Mayo*, Philadelphia Arts Alliance

Living Landscape '94, West Cork Arts Centre, Skibbereen
Arts Fest '94, Regional Technical College, Cork
Claremorris Open Exhibition
Jameson Heritage Centre, Midleton
Íontas, Sligo Art Gallery

1993   *Winners Exhibition*, Claremorris Open Exhibition
Íontas, Sligo Art Gallery
Boyle Arts Festival
Ballinglen Arts Foundation, Ballycastle, Co Mayo

1992   Oireachtas, RHA Gallagher Gallery, Dublin
Living Landscape '92, West Cork Arts Centre, Skibbereen
Íontas, Sligo Art Gallery
Claremorris Open Exhibition
Spirit of Ireland, Narrow Water Gallery, Warrenpoint, Co Down
EV⁺A 92, Limerick City Gallery of Art

1991   *Contemporary Irish Artists*, Syracuse, New York
RHA Annual Exhibition, RHA Gallagher Gallery, Dublin (also 1993, 1994)
Claremorris Open Exhibition
Boyle Arts Festival

1990   Taylor Galleries, Dublin
Vive la Difference, Riverrun Gallery, Limerick
Six Irish Painters, Irish Centre, Brussels

1987   NCAD ten-year retrospective exhibition, Guinness Hop Store, Dublin

Awards

1995   Tyrone Guthrie Centre, Annaghmakerrig (residency)

1994   DHL Artlift Award
Arts Council / Aer Lingus (Artflight)

1993   Ballinglen Arts Foundation, Ballycastle, Co Mayo (fellowship)

1992   Claremorris Open Exhibition (first prize)
Arts Council (materials grant)

1991   RHA Annual Exhibition (Taylor de Vere Award)

Collections

Public Collections – AIB Bank; Contemporary Irish Art Society; Dept of An Taoiseach; King House Collection, Boyle; Office of Public Works; Roscommon County Council

Private Collections – Vincent Ferguson Collection; A & L Goodbody, Dublin; Pat and Antoinette Murphy; and collections in Ireland, Europe, Japan and USA

Mary Lohan is represented by Taylor Galleries, 16 Kildare Street, Dublin 2 (tel: 01-6766055)

GANDON EDITIONS

Gandon Editions is named after the architect James Gandon (1743-1823). In the 1980s, we published occasional titles on art and architecture. In the 1990s, Gandon was formally established as a specialist producer of books on Irish art and architecture. To date, we have produced over 170 titles. Gandon books are available from good bookshops or direct from:

GANDON EDITIONS
Oysterhaven, Kinsale, Co Cork
tel: +353 (0)21 770830 / fax: 770755

PROFILES

In 1996, Gandon Editions launched PROFILES – a series of medium-format books on contemporary Irish art. In 1997, we launched a companion series on Irish architecture. Both series are edited by John O'Regan.

Each volume in the series carries two major texts – an essay and an interview with the artist – and is heavily illustrated in colour. They are of a standard design and pagination, with 48 pages in a 22.5cm square format, and retail at £7.50 paperback.

already published

Profile 1 – PAULINE FLYNN
essays by Paul M O'Reilly and Gus Gibney
ISBN 0946641 722
Gandon Editions, 1996   19 col + 3 b/w illus

Profile 2 – SEÁN McSWEENEY
essay by Brian Fallon
interview by Aidan Dunne
ISBN 0946641 617
Gandon Editions, 1996   17 col + 6 b/w illus

Profile 3 – EILÍS O'CONNELL
essay by Caoimhín Mac Giolla Léith
interview by Medb Ruane
ISBN 0946641 870
Gandon Editions, 1997   27 col + 8 b/w illus

Profile 4 – SIOBÁN PIERCY
essay by Aidan Dunne
interview by Vera Ryan
ISBN 0946641 900
Gandon Editions, 1997   32 col + 6 b/w illus

Profile 5 – MARY LOHAN
introduction by Aidan Dunne
essay by Noel Sheridan
interview by Aidan Dunne
ISBN 0946641 889
Gandon Editions, 1997   col illus

Profile 6 – ALICE MAHER
essay by Medb Ruane
interview by Medb Ruane
ISBN 0946641 935
Gandon Editions, 1997   col illus

to be continued ...